The 'Karen' Phenomenon:

Unmasking the Entitlement Epidemic

A very short introduction by K. R. Stonebridge

The 'Karen' Phenomenon:
Unmasking the Entitlement Epidemic

ISBN: 9798866058334

Printed in the United States of America

Contents

Introduction

Chapter 1:
The Birth of a Meme

Chapter 2:
Historical Precedents

Chapter 3:
The Psychology of a 'Karen'

Chapter 4:
Media's Role

Chapter 5:
Beyond the Gender

Chapter 6:
Racial and Socioeconomic Dimensions

Chapter 7:
The Aftermath

Chapter 8:
Positive Spin-offs

Chapter 9:
Countering the 'Karen' Epidemic

Chapter 10:
The Future of the 'Karen' Phenomenon

Conclusion

Appendix A:
Infamous "Karen" Videos and Their Backstories

Appendix B:
Resources for Further Reading and Understanding

Introduction

Definition and Origin of the Term "Karen"

The term "Karen" has rapidly embedded itself within popular culture, shifting from a simple first name to representing a complex social stereotype. But what precisely does the term imply, and how did this name come to epitomize entitlement and, at times, prejudiced behavior?

What Does "Karen" Mean Today?

"Karen" is a colloquial term used predominantly within Western discourse to typify a certain kind of person—usually a woman—who embodies a specific set of characteristics. These often include entitlement, demand for undue privilege, lack of awareness or sensitivity to others, especially in situations where societal norms or manners would typically prevail. A "Karen" might be seen as someone who, without just cause, asks to "speak to the manager" or who might wield their privilege in ways that are hurtful or dismissive to others.

The Early Beginnings

While it's challenging to pinpoint the exact moment the name "Karen" began its cultural transformation, there are identifiable moments of genesis. Comedian Dane Cook, in a 2005 stand-up routine, depicted "Karen" as "that friend nobody likes." While Cook's description doesn't entirely encapsulate the contemporary understanding of a "Karen," it was an early example of the name being used in a pejorative sense.

The vast expanses of internet forums and social media platforms further pushed the narrative. On Reddit, stories emerged where users described encounters with entitled individuals, dubbing them "Karen" in the process. Memes, the modern hieroglyphics of internet culture, began to proliferate, showcasing scenarios like "Karen took the kids," emphasizing her as an unreasonably demanding ex-wife.

"Can I Speak to the Manager?"

Perhaps the most iconic representation of the "Karen" stereotype revolves around her alleged proclivity to demand to "speak to the manager" over minor grievances. This paints a picture of a woman, often depicted with a bob haircut, ready to escalate trivial issues or expecting preferential treatment, especially in consumer-based scenarios. It's a scene many working in the service industry have lamentably experienced. While it remains murky as to where this portrayal first originated, it struck a chord due to its widespread relatability, embedding the "Karen" character firmly in popular consciousness.

The Socio-Cultural Dimension: Race and Privilege

Recent years have added layers to the "Karen" persona. Amidst the backdrop of rising consciousness around racial injustices, the term started being employed in situations highlighting racial ignorance or prejudice. Social media channels were awash with videos showcasing white women, quickly branded as "Karens," making unwarranted calls to the police on Black individuals for minor, often fabricated transgressions. This amplified dimension of racial bias attached a heavier weight to the term, evolving it from a meme to a potent commentary on societal privilege and prejudice.

Gender, Ageism, and Controversy

As with any stereotype, the term "Karen" is a double-edged sword. Critics argue that it's ageist, focusing unfairly on middle-aged women, and sexist, targeting women more than men. The moniker "Ken" has been proposed for male counterparts, but it hasn't gained as much traction, emphasizing the gendered nature of the criticism.

However, proponents believe the term has value in spotlighting behaviors that reflect entitlement, privilege, or racial bias. In their view, it's less about the name and more about the actions and attitudes it critiques. This debate underscores the term's complexity and the broader discussions it sparks about societal behaviors and attitudes.

The Power of Names and Identity

The evolution of "Karen" offers a fascinating study into how names, free from their initial personal identity connotations, can morph into powerful social commentaries. Names like "Debbie Downer" or "Negative Nancy" have had similar trajectories, albeit without the racial connotations. Such transformations underscore the influence of collective societal experiences and the mediums of culture—be it stand-up routines or meme formats—in shaping language.

In diving into the depths of the "Karen" phenomenon, it's vital to remember the individuality and humanity of the many people named Karen, who don't fit this stereotype. Their experiences, often marred by the negative connotations of the term, serve as a reminder of the broader implications of societal labels.

As we navigate the following chapters, we aim to understand the "Karen" phenomenon in all its dimensions, exploring its roots, its implications, and its impact on both individual and collective identities.

Overview of the Book's Structure and Aims

The phenomenon surrounding the term "Karen" offers a rich tapestry of social, cultural, and psychological insights. Through this book, we aspire not only to trace the origins and evolution of the term but also to delve deeper into the societal underpinnings that have allowed such a term to flourish and become embedded within contemporary discourse. Here, we outline the structure of the book and its overarching aims to provide clarity on our journey ahead.

Chapter Breakdown

Chapter 1: The Birth of a Meme

Our journey starts with tracing the roots. We delve into the early mentions of "Karen" in its derogatory sense, from comedy sketches to the vast corridors of online forums, illustrating its initial transformation from a name to a cultural signifier.

Chapter 2: Historical Precedents

Understanding "Karen" requires a broader historical context. We examine the stereotypes of demanding and entitled women throughout history, weaving a thread between past narratives and today's "Karen" archetype.

Chapter 3: The Psychology of a 'Karen'

Beyond the memes and jokes lies a realm of psychological insights. Why do some people exhibit "Karen-like" behaviors? What societal or individual triggers might exist? This chapter delves into the mindset and possible motivations.

Chapter 4: Media's Role

In our digital age, media acts as a catalyst. We explore how various platforms, from news outlets to social media, amplify "Karen" incidents and the repercussions of such amplification.

Chapter 5: Beyond the Gender

While "Karen" primarily targets women, entitled behavior isn't gender-specific. We discuss the male counterparts and examine the gender dynamics at play, offering a more holistic view of entitlement in society.

Chapter 6: Racial and Socioeconomic Dimensions

The term "Karen" isn't just about entitlement—it has racial undertones too. We dissect instances where racial prejudice comes to the fore, linking them to broader societal issues.

Chapter 7: The Aftermath

Being labeled a "Karen" in the internet age can have severe real-world consequences. This chapter looks at the aftermath of such incidents, exploring themes of public shaming, redemption, and personal growth.

Chapter 8: Positive Spin-offs

Every cloud has a silver lining. We bring to light stories where individuals turned their "Karen" moments into self-awareness opportunities and the communities that fostered such transformation.

Chapter 9: Countering the 'Karen' Epidemic

For every action, there's a reaction. We present strategies and stories of those who've successfully diffused "Karen" situations, offering readers tools to handle similar scenarios.

Chapter 10: The Future of the 'Karen' Phenomenon

What lies ahead for "Karen"? We speculate on the meme's trajectory and its potential long-term implications for societal discourse.

Aims of the Book

1. **Educate and Inform**: This book seeks to provide readers with a comprehensive understanding of the "Karen" phenomenon, dissecting its layers and nuances.

2. **Promote Empathy and Understanding**: While it's easy to mock or dismiss "Karens," our aim is to foster empathy. By understanding the factors that lead to such behaviors, we hope to encourage more compassionate responses.

3. **Stimulate Discussion**: The term "Karen" touches on broader societal issues, from gender dynamics to racial prejudice. We hope this book acts as a catalyst for deeper conversations about these critical subjects.

4. **Provide Guidance**: For those encountering "Karen" behaviors, we offer strategies and insights to handle such situations constructively.

In this exploration, we hope to offer a balanced, comprehensive, and insightful view of the "Karen" phenomenon, situating it within broader societal contexts and offering pathways for understanding, discussion, and growth.

Chapter 1:
The Birth of a Meme

Tracing back the first instances of the "Karen" meme

The digital age has seen countless trends rise and fall, but few have garnered as much attention and simultaneous controversy as the "Karen" meme. An emblematic representation of entitlement and privilege, "Karen" has evolved from a simple meme to a social commentary. To fully grasp the phenomenon's depth, it's crucial to embark on a retrospective journey, tracing its roots and understanding its initial ascendancy.

Humble Comedic Beginnings

Before the term took the internet by storm, the name "Karen" was given a light-hearted, if not entirely flattering, spotlight in comedy. Dane Cook, in his 2005 stand-up routine, humorously depicted "Karen" as the proverbial "friend that nobody likes." While Cook's portrayal wasn't a complete match with the meme's later characteristics, it was an early instance of the name "Karen" being used in a pejorative context. This comedic inception, whether directly influential or not, sowed the seeds for what was to emerge in later years.

The Flourishing of "Karen" on Internet Forums

The true catalyst for "Karen" as a meme, however, came from the vast and intricate world of internet forums. By the late 2010s, platforms like Reddit became breeding grounds for "Karen" stories. These tales often involved middle-aged women, depicted as entitled or unaware, stirring unnecessary drama or making unreasonable demands. The narrative seemed consistent: a woman, often named Karen for convenience or comedic value, would embody all the undesirable traits that people had encountered in real-life interactions.

The Reddit community, ever eager to craft narratives, didn't stop at mere stories. Subreddits such as r/FuckYouKaren gained traction, with users exchanging "Karen" memes, anecdotes, and jokes. One particularly viral meme format portrayed "Karen" as a difficult ex-wife, with phrases like "Karen took the kids" becoming internet catchphrases. This narrative painted Karen not just as entitled but also as vindictive, further adding layers to the burgeoning stereotype.

Iconic Characteristics: Haircut, Attitude, and The Manager

As the meme matured, so did its associated imagery. The "Karen haircut," often a distinct angled bob—shorter at the back and longer at the front—became emblematic of the stereotype. This specific hairstyle, whether fairly or not, began to symbolize the "Karen" attitude, reinforcing the trope every time someone spotted a similar haircut in real life.

Furthermore, "Karen's" disposition was crystalized with the frequently cited demand to "speak to the manager." This scenario, familiar to many working in customer service, epitomized her lack of patience, her sense of entitlement, and her penchant for escalation. The "Karen" meme was no longer just about a name or a haircut—it encapsulated a specific kind of disruptive behavior, especially evident in retail or dining contexts.

Life Imitates Art: Real-world "Karens"

What set the "Karen" meme apart from many fleeting internet jokes was its grounding in real-life encounters. As the meme gained prominence, videos and stories began emerging online, showcasing individuals—predominantly women—exhibiting behavior that matched the "Karen" archetype. These real-world "Karens," whether caught making unwarranted 911 calls or berating service workers without cause, were instantly labeled as such by the online community.

These instances not only reinforced the meme but also began shaping its narrative. Every video or story added nuance, sometimes introducing racial prejudice or other biases, transforming "Karen" from a light-hearted meme into a more profound social critique.

Societal Reflections and the Power of Shared Experience

The "Karen" meme's ascendancy can't be credited solely to catchy internet jokes or isolated video clips. Its strength lay in the shared experiences of millions. From service industry workers to bystanders witnessing entitled behavior, many could relate to the "Karen" narrative, making it a powerful and resonant trope. In essence, the meme served as a mirror, reflecting widespread societal encounters back to the masses, but with a humorous, meme-infused twist.

In Retrospect

Tracing the origins and evolution of the "Karen" meme provides valuable insights into how internet culture interacts with, and often amplifies, societal perceptions and stereotypes. From a comedic quip to a defining meme, and further into a symbol of entitlement and privilege, "Karen" showcases the fluidity and dynamism of digital-era narratives. As we proceed, we'll delve deeper into the complexities and implications of this phenomenon, unraveling its multi-faceted dimensions one layer at a time.

Analyzing the Social Factors that Gave Rise to the "Karen" Phenomenon

In dissecting the roots of the "Karen" meme, it becomes evident that its ascent wasn't merely a spontaneous digital occurrence. Instead, it was fueled and shaped by a variety of social factors. This chapter delves into the societal elements that played a role in giving birth to and elevating the "Karen" narrative.

A Desire for Collective Catharsis

Many people have encountered individuals in their lives who displayed an air of unjustified entitlement or who behaved in a confrontational manner over seemingly trivial matters. The "Karen" meme served as a collective repository for such experiences, granting individuals an outlet to vent, share, and laugh about these shared encounters. The meme's ubiquity and popularity reveal a widespread desire for a collective catharsis — a way for society to express its frustration and humorously mock behaviors deemed undesirable.

The Service Industry's Silent Cry

With a significant portion of the population working in the service industry, there's a vast reservoir of experiences with demanding and difficult customers. For many service workers, the "Karen" meme became a symbol of their daily struggles, encapsulating those customers who made their jobs particularly challenging. The meme served as a subtle form of protest, a silent cry against the thankless aspects of customer service, allowing workers to bond over shared challenges.

Digital Amplification of Anecdotal Experiences

The digital age, marked by the proliferation of smartphones and social media, has facilitated the rapid sharing of personal experiences. Incidents that might have once remained confined to one's close circle are now broadcast to the world, amplifying anecdotal experiences. Every video or story of a real-world "Karen" not only validated the meme but also fueled its growth. The immediate virality of these incidents showcased the resonance of the "Karen" narrative, turning isolated episodes into widely recognized phenomena.

A Response to Societal Privilege

The "Karen" meme, while humorous on the surface, touches on deeper societal issues, especially concerning privilege. "Karens" are often portrayed as taking advantage of their perceived societal status, wielding it inappropriately or unjustly. This meme, in many ways, became a critique of unchecked privilege, mocking those who blatantly misuse it. It's no coincidence that many "Karen" episodes involve racial or class biases, as the meme intersects with broader social critiques about who holds power in society and how it's wielded.

Gender Dynamics and Stereotypes

While the "Karen" phenomenon predominantly targets women, it can't be divorced from broader gender dynamics. Historically, women have been the subject of various stereotypes — some positive, others negative. The "Karen" meme, in some ways, plays into age-old tropes of the "hysterical woman" or the "nagging wife." Its popularity underscores the tensions and expectations surrounding female behavior in public spaces, where assertiveness can quickly be misconstrued as aggression or entitlement.

The Desire for Simplified Archetypes

Humans have an inherent desire to categorize and label, simplifying complex phenomena into easily digestible archetypes. The "Karen" meme serves this function, offering a recognizable label for a particular set of behaviors. By assigning a name and a set of characteristics to this behavior, society can more easily discuss, critique, and joke about it. This simplification, however, also carries risks, as it can lead to over-generalization and unjust labeling.

The Need for Humor in Tense Times

The rise of the "Karen" meme also coincides with particularly tense and polarized times, marked by political divisions, social unrest, and a global pandemic. In such periods, humor becomes a crucial coping mechanism. The "Karen" meme, with its blend of satire, humor, and social critique, provides a light-hearted escape from heavier issues, even as it touches upon them.

In Conclusion

The "Karen" meme's emergence is a confluence of social desires, frustrations, and observations. It stands as a testament to society's need to label, critique, and find humor in shared experiences, while also highlighting deeper issues of privilege, gender dynamics, and societal expectations. As we navigate this intricate landscape, it's crucial to recognize both the meme's comedic value and its profound societal implications, understanding that behind every viral trend lies a tapestry of human experiences, emotions, and critiques.

Chapter 2: Historical Precedents

The Stereotypes of Demanding and Entitled Women Throughout History

The "Karen" meme, though a product of our digital age, is not the first instance where women have been labeled as demanding or entitled. History is rife with examples where female assertiveness was misconstrued as undue entitlement, and where women's demands were viewed with suspicion or derision. This chapter explores these historical stereotypes, shedding light on how perceptions of women have evolved and how past prejudices have influenced contemporary narratives.

The "Temperamental" Queens and Noblewomen

Throughout history, particularly in patriarchal societies, powerful women were often portrayed as temperamental or capricious. Queens like Marie Antoinette of France were criticized and satirized for their alleged extravagance and insensitivity to the common people. Whether or not these depictions were accurate, they served political purposes, undermining these women's authority and casting doubts on their ability to rule.

The "Hysterical" Woman

The term "hysteria," derived from the Greek word for uterus, was historically used to describe a medical condition thought to be particular to women. Symptoms ranged from nervousness to outspokenness, and its "diagnosis" served as a convenient tool to dismiss women's emotions, demands, or grievances. This stereotype painted women as inherently unstable, their desires and demands as irrational, and provided a medical basis for silencing them.

The Suffragettes: "Demanding" the Right to Vote

The early 20th century saw the rise of the suffragette movement, where women across the globe campaigned for their right to vote. These women, passionate and assertive, were often portrayed by their opponents as aggressively demanding, disrupting the societal order, and overstepping their "natural" roles. Cartoons of the era often exaggerated these stereotypes, showing suffragettes as neglectful mothers or domineering wives.

The "Gold Digger" Trope

The Jazz Age and the subsequent decades witnessed the popularization of the "gold digger" stereotype — women who sought relationships with men solely for monetary gain. These women were often portrayed in films, literature, and the media as manipulative, entitled, and opportunistic. This stereotype perpetuated the idea that women were primarily driven by materialistic desires and would go to any lengths to secure a luxurious lifestyle.

The Modern "Diva"

Popular culture in the late 20th and early 21st century introduced the trope of the "diva." While the term originally referred to celebrated female opera singers, its contemporary usage often denotes a woman who is seen as high-maintenance, demanding, and difficult to please. Pop stars, actresses, and other celebrities have frequently been labeled as "divas" in media portrayals, emphasizing their supposed entitlement or unreasonable demands.

Subverting Stereotypes: Women's Liberation Movement

The 1960s and 70s witnessed the Women's Liberation Movement, a concerted effort to challenge and change societal norms around gender. Women demanded equal rights, challenged established norms, and sought to reclaim narratives that had historically been used against them. While this movement made significant strides in changing perceptions, it also faced backlash. Many assertive women, standing up against discrimination, were labeled as overly aggressive, shrill, or entitled — a precursor to today's "Karen" stereotype.

The Underlying Theme: Fear of Female Autonomy

A common thread runs through these historical precedents: the societal discomfort with women asserting themselves, making demands, or stepping out of their prescribed roles. Whether it's a queen making political decisions, a woman demanding her right to vote, or a female celebrity setting boundaries, history often cast these women as disruptive, entitled, or irrational. These portrayals reflect a broader societal unease with female autonomy and agency.

Concluding Thoughts

Understanding the historical context of the "Karen" meme and its predecessors is crucial. It offers insights into how women's behaviors have been perceived and judged throughout history, often through a lens of bias and patriarchal expectations. As the "Karen" meme continues to evolve, it's essential to approach it with a nuanced perspective, informed by the weight of historical precedents and the recognition of the broader societal forces at play.

How These Stereotypes Have Changed or Remained Constant

While the essence of the "Karen" meme may feel distinctly modern, the underlying stereotypes it taps into have roots that stretch far back into history. To understand its full context, it's essential to examine how these age-old stereotypes of demanding and entitled women have morphed over time — and crucially, how certain facets have stubbornly remained constant.

The Ebb and Flow of Queenly Portrayals

Historically, powerful female rulers were frequently painted as volatile or capricious, their assertiveness interpreted as a sign of inherent instability. But as time progressed and feminist movements championed the reassessment of history, these portrayals started to shift. Today, figures like Queen Elizabeth I or Cleopatra are often celebrated for their leadership and political acumen. However, even in contemporary media, the trope of the 'mad queen,' as epitomized by characters like Cersei Lannister in "Game of Thrones," reveals the persistence of this stereotype.

From "Hysteria" to Mental Health Awareness

The concept of female "hysteria" has largely been debunked and is viewed as a dark chapter in the history of medicine and gender relations. With the advancement of psychology and psychiatry, coupled with women's rights movements, there's been a more comprehensive understanding of women's mental health. None-theless, echoes of the 'hysterical' stereotype linger. Women are still often dismissed as being "overly emotional" or "irrational," especial-ly when expressing strong opinions or grievances.

Suffragettes to Modern Activists

While the suffragettes were once derided as aggressively demand-ing, today, they're celebrated as trailblazers in the fight for gender equality. Their methods and messages have inspired countless oth-er movements. Yet, when contemporary women take to the streets to advocate for their rights, they often face the same criticisms. Activists, whether they're campaigning for gender equality, racial justice, or climate action, frequently confront claims that they're being "too loud," "too emotional," or "too demanding."

The "Gold Digger" Evolves

The "gold digger" stereotype has evolved but hasn't disappeared. In the age of prenups and high-profile celebrity divorces, the trope persists, suggesting that some women are only in relationships for financial gain. However, recent pop culture also sees this stereo-type being reclaimed or subverted. Songs like Kanye West's "Gold Digger" or films that play with this trope often portray women as strategic and empowered, if not entirely free from judgment.

Divas and Influencers

The modern "diva" of the late 20th century, often seen as a woman with grandiose demands, has found her 21st-century counterpart in the influencer — particularly those characterized as being out of touch or entitled. While some influencers are celebrated for their savvy, others are criticized for their perceived vanity and materialism, showing that society's discomfort with women who don't conform to expectations of humility and modesty endures.

Women's Liberation and the Backlash

The Women's Liberation Movement made monumental strides in reshaping societal perceptions of women. Still, the backlash it faced wasn't entirely left in the 20th century. Today, women who advocate for gender equality, especially those who do so vociferously, often confront derogatory labels. Terms like "feminazi" — a portmanteau of feminist and Nazi — are used to discredit and mock their efforts, revealing the enduring discomfort with women who challenge the status quo.

The Enduring Fear of Female Autonomy

While the forms and specifics of the stereotypes have morphed, an underlying theme persists: a deep-seated unease with women who assert themselves outside of prescribed norms. Whether it's a woman asserting her political power, seeking financial independence, demanding respect, or simply asking to be heard, she risks being labeled as disruptive, aggressive, or entitled.

In Summation

The "Karen" meme, with its undertones of entitlement and unreasonableness, taps into a rich tapestry of historical stereotypes about women. Yet, its modern iteration also offers an opportunity for reflection. By understanding how these stereotypes have evolved — and recognizing where they've remained stubbornly constant — society can better address the biases that persist today. The hope is that with awareness, reflection, and active effort, the next chapters in gender relations will be marked by understanding and equality, rather than rehashed stereotypes.

Chapter 3: The Psychology of a 'Karen'

Exploring the Mindset and Motivations of Those Who Display "Karen-like" Behavior

At the heart of the "Karen" meme lies a stereotype — an individual displaying an exaggerated sense of entitlement, often combined with aggressive demands and a lack of empathy towards others. But beyond the viral videos and social media commentary, what drives individuals to act in such a manner? What psychological factors underpin "Karen-like" behavior? This chapter delves deeper into the mindset and motivations of such individuals.

A Quest for Control

One of the defining features of "Karen-like" behavior is a strong desire for control. This could arise from various factors:

- **Insecurity:** A person might attempt to control their environment or other people as a way to manage their own internal insecurities.

- **Past Trauma:** Experiences of feeling powerless or out of control in the past might lead to overcompensating behaviors in the present.

- **Learned Behavior:** Growing up in environments where control and assertiveness were rewarded might condition individuals to employ these tactics in adulthood.

Entitlement: Real vs. Perceived

The sense of entitlement, another hallmark of the "Karen" archetype, can be rooted in:

- **Cultural Conditioning:** In societies that promote individualism, people might be conditioned to prioritize their needs and rights over communal harmony.
- **Socio-economic Status:** Coming from privileged backgrounds can sometimes create blind spots, leading individuals to expect preferential treatment based on their socio-economic standing.
- **Past Experiences:** Repeated instances where one's demands or desires were readily met can condition an expectation for similar treatment in various scenarios.

A Lack of Emotional Regulation

The aggressive and confrontational aspect of "Karen-like" behavior indicates difficulties in emotional regulation. Such individuals might:

- **React impulsively** without considering the consequences of their actions.
- **Struggle to manage strong emotions,** leading to outbursts or aggressive confrontations.
- **Lack coping strategies** for dealing with frustration, leading them to externalize their feelings.

Cognitive Biases at Play

Certain cognitive biases can feed into "Karen-like" behaviors:

- **Confirmation Bias:** Once someone has formed a belief (e.g., "I am always right"), they may only seek out information that confirms this belief, disregarding contradictory evidence.
- **Superiority Bias:** The belief that one's opinions, beliefs, or status are superior to others can lead to dismissive and condescending behaviors.

- **Bias Blind Spot:** This is the inability to recognize that one's own judgment is impacted by biases, leading to an inflated self-perception.

Social Reinforcements

Sometimes, "Karen-like" behaviors are reinforced, either directly or indirectly:

- **Attention:** In an age of social media, confrontations can attract attention, and for some, negative attention is better than no attention.
- **Getting Desired Outcomes:** If aggressive demands frequently result in getting one's way — due to others wanting to avoid conflict — the behavior is inadvertently reinforced.
- **In-group Validation:** If individuals surround themselves with like-minded people who validate their actions and views, it can embolden their behaviors.

The Role of Empathy (or lack thereof)

Empathy, the ability to understand and share the feelings of another, seems to be in short supply in many "Karen" incidents. This lack might stem from:

- **Narrow Social Circles:** Limited exposure to diverse perspectives can hinder the development of empathy.
- **Desensitization:** Repeated exposure to conflict or confrontational scenarios, especially online, can lead to a diminished empathetic response.
- **Cognitive Overload:** In our fast-paced world, cognitive burnout might reduce one's capacity for empathy, leading to self-centered behaviors.

Concluding Reflections

While it's tempting to simplify the "Karen" phenomenon as mere entitlement or rudeness, a deeper exploration reveals a complex interplay of psychological factors. It's essential to approach the topic with nuance and avoid painting all individuals displaying "Karen-like" behaviors with a broad brush.

Understanding the underpinnings of such behaviors provides an opportunity for societal reflection. By addressing these root causes — whether it's promoting emotional intelligence in education, encouraging diverse interactions, or challenging cognitive biases — we can hope to foster a society marked by understanding and collaboration rather than confrontation.

Examining the Intersection of Entitlement, Privilege, and Ignorance

The "Karen" phenomenon is multi-faceted, with entitlement, privilege, and ignorance often interwoven in complex ways. This section endeavors to explore how these components intersect and amplify one another, resulting in the behaviors commonly associated with the "Karen" archetype.

The Roots of Entitlement

Entitlement, at its core, is the belief that one inherently deserves certain privileges or treatment. This belief can manifest in various ways:

- **Past Experience:** Repeated instances where demands or wishes are met can foster an expectation for similar treatment across diverse scenarios.

- **Social Validation:** Being in environments where one's views are constantly validated can lead to an inflated sense of self-worth.

- **Cultural Conditioning:** In societies valuing individual rights and freedoms, a heightened sense of personal entitlement can sometimes overshadow communal or collective needs.

Privilege: The Unseen Advantage

Privilege refers to the unearned advantages or exemptions some individuals enjoy based purely on aspects of their identity, such as race, gender, or socio-economic status. Its manifestations can be subtle, often invisible to those who possess it. The relation between privilege and "Karen-like" behavior can be outlined as:

- **Blind Spots:** Privilege can lead to a lack of awareness about the challenges and experiences of those without the same advantages.

- **Expectation of Preferential Treatment:** Individuals accustomed to privilege might expect the world to accommodate them, resulting in confrontations when their expectations are not met.

- **Defense Mechanisms:** Recognizing one's privilege can be uncomfortable. Some might respond defensively when their privilege is pointed out, leading to "Karen-like" confrontations.

Ignorance: The Fuel to the Fire

Ignorance, in this context, is not merely a lack of knowledge but an active resistance to understanding or recognizing the perspectives and experiences of others. This plays a role in the "Karen" archetype by:

- **Reinforcing Biases:** Without exposure to diverse perspectives, individuals can become entrenched in their beliefs, further distancing themselves from understanding others.

- **Blocking Empathy:** Ignorance can act as a barrier to empathy, making it hard for individuals to connect with or understand those from different backgrounds.

- **Escalating Confrontations:** A lack of awareness or understanding can lead to misinterpretations, causing minor disagreements to blow up into full-blown confrontations.

The Entwined Trio

The real power of these three elements — entitlement, privilege, and ignorance — lies in their capacity to reinforce one another:

1. **Entitlement and Privilege:** Entitlement can stem from privilege. Those with societal advantages might come to expect certain treatments or accommodations based on their previous experiences. When these expectations are challenged, the resulting confrontations become emblematic of the "Karen" archetype.

2. **Privilege and Ignorance:** The insulating effect of privilege can lead to ignorance. Those not accustomed to facing challenges or disadvantages might remain unaware of systemic issues, leading to a lack of understanding or even dismissal of the experiences of others.

3. **Ignorance and Entitlement:** Entitlement, when fueled by ignorance, becomes particularly problematic. Individuals might feel they deserve certain treatment without understanding the broader context, leading to demands that seem unreasonable or out of touch.

The Societal Implications

The intersection of entitlement, privilege, and ignorance has broader societal implications. It highlights systemic issues that allow certain groups to remain insulated from the realities faced by others. Furthermore, the confrontations and behaviors resulting from this intersection can further deepen divides, creating an environment where dialogue and understanding become increasingly challenging.

Moving Forward

To address the behaviors associated with the "Karen" archetype, it's crucial to understand and tackle the underlying factors of entitlement, privilege, and ignorance. This requires:

- **Education:** Broader and more inclusive education can challenge ignorance, offering insights into diverse perspectives and experiences.

- **Self-reflection:** Individuals must be willing to examine their own privilege and entitlement, recognizing where they might have blind spots.

- **Open Dialogue:** Encouraging environments where people can discuss and confront their biases and beliefs can pave the way for greater understanding and empathy.

Conclusion

The "Karen" phenomenon, while often presented humorously or with scorn, offers a mirror to societal dynamics. By delving into the psychology behind these behaviors, society can hope to address the root causes, fostering a future marked by understanding, collaboration, and mutual respect.

Chapter 4: Media's Role

How Media, Including Social Platforms, Amplify "Karen" Incidents

In our digital age, media—especially social platforms—serve as powerful amplifiers for various phenomena, including the "Karen" incidents. The spread and evolution of the "Karen" meme, from a humorous jab to a cultural critique, owe much to the role of media. This chapter examines how these platforms spotlight, shape, and sometimes even exacerbate "Karen" behaviors.

The Virality Factor

One of the defining characteristics of modern media is its potential for virality. A single incident, captured on video, can quickly garner millions of views, comments, and shares.

- **Instant Gratification:** Social platforms are designed for quick consumption and sharing. A catchy video title like "Karen loses it at a grocery store" is likely to attract clicks and shares due to human curiosity and the desire for entertainment.

- **Echo Chambers:** Social media algorithms often push content that aligns with a user's pre-existing beliefs or interests. This can result in a feedback loop, where similar "Karen" incidents continuously pop up in a user's feed, giving an impression of their ubiquity.

The Role of Outrage Culture

Modern media, especially social platforms, thrives on emotions—and outrage is among the most potent. "Karen" incidents, which often showcase overt entitlement or prejudice, naturally invoke strong reactions.

- **Shared Indignation:** When viewers witness seemingly unjust behavior, they're compelled to share it, hoping to rally others to their cause or viewpoint.

- **Call-Out Culture:** Social media provides a platform for users to call out perceived wrongs. Publicly shaming individuals, including "Karens," can serve as both a deterrent and a form of social justice in the eyes of many.

- **The Snowball Effect:** As an incident gains traction, it often attracts comments and reactions from influencers or celebrities, further amplifying its reach.

Media's Role in Shaping Perception

While media provides a spotlight, it also influences how incidents are perceived:

- **Narrative Framing:** The way a story or incident is presented can shape viewers' opinions. A video clip might be edited to emphasize certain parts, while others are left out, potentially skewing the full context.

- **Meme-fication:** Turning incidents into memes or catchy hashtags simplifies complex issues. While it aids spread and recall, it can also reduce nuanced understanding.

- **Feedback Loop:** As "Karen" videos become popular, more individuals might actively seek or provoke such incidents hoping to capture the next viral sensation.

The Double-Edged Sword of Public Scrutiny

The widespread dissemination of "Karen" incidents has both positive and negative repercussions:

- **Accountability:** Public exposure can lead to real-world consequences. "Karens" might face social backlash, job loss, or other repercussions, serving as a deterrent for similar behavior.

- **Overexposure:** The constant barrage of such incidents can lead to desensitization. What once invoked outrage can become just another video in the feed.

- **Potential for Misjudgment:** Without the full context, viewers might rush to judgment. Individuals labeled as "Karens" might sometimes be dealing with personal issues, mental health challenges, or other factors that the viral clip doesn't capture.

A Reflection of Society's Values and Biases

Media, in all its forms, is a mirror to society, reflecting and amplifying its values, beliefs, and biases:

- **Spotlight on Entitlement and Prejudice:** The popularity of "Karen" incidents highlights societal disdain for unchecked privilege and overt prejudice.
- **Gender Dynamics:** The term "Karen" is gendered, and its virality raises questions about societal perceptions of assertive or confrontational women. While male equivalents exist (e.g., "Ken" or "Kevin"), the "Karen" meme's prominence might indicate underlying gender biases.
- **Racial Undertones:** Many viral "Karen" incidents involve confrontations with individuals of color, bringing to the forefront issues of racial bias and systemic racism. The media's portrayal and public's reception of these incidents offer insights into broader societal dynamics.

Conclusion

Media, especially in its modern, digital form, plays a pivotal role in the spread, perception, and impact of "Karen" incidents. While it offers a platform for accountability and social critique, it also poses challenges, including potential for misjudgment and overexposure. As consumers of media, recognizing its influence and potential biases is crucial to foster understanding and bridge divides.

The Dangers of Online Mob Mentality

As the digital age progresses, the power of the online collective grows. Social platforms, while fostering connectivity, can sometimes create environments conducive to the rise of online mob mentality. The fervor with which online communities can rally around or against a cause, individual, or incident is unprecedented. Understanding the dangers of this online behavior is crucial to navigating the digital space responsibly and ethically.

The Anatomy of Online Mobs

Online mobs, sometimes called "cybermobs," are large groups of Internet users who band together around a common cause or target. Their rise can be attributed to:

- **Anonymity:** Online platforms often allow users to hide behind pseudonyms or anonymous profiles, emboldening them to act without fear of real-world consequences.
- **Instant Communication:** The immediacy of online communication means information (or misinformation) can spread rapidly.
- **Groupthink:** Online spaces, especially echo chambers, foster environments where dissenting opinions are suppressed, leading to a homogeneous set of beliefs.

The Risks of Rapid Reaction

One of the defining characteristics of online mobs is the swiftness with which they form and act. This rapidity, however, can lead to:

- **Rushed Judgments:** Without taking the time to verify information or understand context, mobs can target innocent individuals or exacerbate situations based on half-truths.
- **Escalation:** A small incident can quickly blow out of proportion, with thousands or even millions rallying around a cause without fully understanding its nuances.
- **Permanent Consequences:** In the digital age, the Internet never forgets. Targets of online mobs can face lasting repercussions, from damaged reputations to mental health challenges.

Amplification of Extreme Views

Online mob mentality can push moderate views to the extremes:

- **Polarization:** As opposing sides clash, middle-ground perspectives get drowned out, leading to a binary "us vs. them" scenario.

- **Reinforcement of Beliefs:** Within echo chambers, extreme views can be continuously reinforced, making them seem more mainstream than they actually are.

- **Dehumanization:** Extreme views often dehumanize the opposing side, making it easier for online mobs to justify attacks or harassment.

The Impact on Individual Targets

Individuals at the receiving end of online mob mentality can face dire consequences:

- **Doxxing:** The malicious act of revealing private information about an individual online can lead to real-world threats, harassment, or harm.

- **Mental Health Strains:** Being targeted by an online mob can lead to anxiety, depression, or even suicidal thoughts.

- **Career and Personal Repercussions:** Targets can lose jobs, relationships, and face ostracization based on online mob actions.

The Societal Ramifications

Beyond individual targets, the rise of online mob mentality has broader societal implications:

- **Stifled Dialogue:** Fear of backlash can prevent individuals from voicing opinions, leading to a lack of diverse perspectives and stifled public discourse.

- **Misinformation:** As online mobs spread unverified or out-of-context information, society's understanding of events, individuals, or issues can be skewed.

- **Desensitization:** As online mob actions become more common, society might become desensitized to their dangers, normalizing harmful behaviors.

Navigating and Combating Mob Mentality

Understanding the dangers of online mob mentality is the first step. Combatting its rise requires:

- **Education:** Digital literacy programs can teach users to verify information, understand biases, and engage online ethically.

- **Platform Responsibility:** Social media platforms can implement stricter regulations, algorithms, or interventions to prevent the rapid spread of misinformation or curb online harassment.

- **Promote Empathy:** Online actions have real-world consequences. Humanizing online interactions and understanding the person behind the screen can deter mob behavior.

- **Encourage Critical Thinking:** Fostering an online culture that values critical thinking over blind allegiance can challenge the rise of mob mentality.

Conclusion

The power of the collective is a double-edged sword. While online communities can rally for positive change, the rise of mob mentality poses real dangers to individuals and society. Recognizing these dangers, coupled with proactive education and platform interventions, can pave the way for a more ethical and empathetic digital age.

Chapter 5: Beyond the Gender

Addressing the Term's Inherent Gender Bias

The "Karen" meme, while offering social commentary on entitlement and ignorance, is not devoid of its own complications, particularly when it comes to gender. At its heart, the term carries an inherent gender bias, linking specific negative behaviors predominantly to women. This chapter delves deep into the gendered nuances of the "Karen" phenomenon, aiming to shed light on its implications and the broader gender dynamics at play.

The Gendered Nature of "Karen"

The term "Karen" specifically targets women. While there have been attempts to create male counterparts with names like "Ken" or "Kevin," none have reached the same level of virality or cultural significance as "Karen." This disparity raises essential questions:

- **Why Women?** Why has society predominantly associated these behaviors with women? Is it a reflection of deeper-seated beliefs or biases about how women should behave?

- **The Power of Names:** Names carry weight and history. By associating negative behaviors with a common female name, the meme inadvertently casts a shadow on countless individuals named Karen, regardless of their behavior.

Historical Gender Stereotypes

The "Karen" meme doesn't exist in isolation. It's an evolution of age-old stereotypes that have persisted for centuries:

- **The Nagging Woman:** Historically, assertive or vocal women have been labeled as nagging, bothersome, or hysterical.

These labels, deeply entrenched in patriarchal systems, serve to diminish women's voices and concerns.

- **The Irrational Female:** The stereotype of women as overly emotional or irrational has been used to undermine their authority and decision-making capabilities.

The "Karen" phenomenon, in many ways, builds upon these stereotypes, presenting women as unreasonable, entitled, or overbearing.

Implications for Modern Women

Modern women, even those far removed from the "Karen" stereotype, face the repercussions of the meme:

- **Silencing Voices:** Fear of being labeled a "Karen" might deter women from voicing legitimate concerns or standing up for themselves.

- **Double Standards:** Men displaying similar behaviors might not face the same level of scrutiny or backlash, leading to gendered double standards.

- **Misrepresentation:** Not every woman labeled as a "Karen" is necessarily entitled or ignorant. The label, in its oversimplified form, can misrepresent complex situations or behaviors.

Moving Beyond Gender

To address the gender bias inherent in the "Karen" term, society needs to:

- **Acknowledge the Bias:** Recognizing the gendered nature of the meme is the first step. By accepting that it carries gender biases, individuals can start to question its usage and implications.

- **Humanize, Not Label:** Instead of resorting to labels, understanding the human behind the behavior is essential. People, regardless of gender, have complex motivations, backgrounds, and experiences that influence their actions.

- **Promote Gender-Neutral Critiques:** If the aim is to critique entitlement, ignorance, or prejudice, using gender-neutral terms or approaches ensures that the focus remains on behavior rather than gender.

Intersectionality: Gender and Beyond

The "Karen" meme, while predominantly gendered, also touches upon other social dimensions:

- **Race:** Many "Karen" incidents involve confrontations with individuals of color, indicating racial undertones. This intersection of gender and race complicates the meme further, with white women sometimes weaponizing their gender and race against individuals of color.
- **Class:** The entitled behavior associated with "Karens" often comes with an undercurrent of class privilege, suggesting that these individuals believe their socio-economic status grants them certain rights or superiority.

Recognizing these intersections is crucial, as they provide a richer understanding of the dynamics at play, ensuring that critiques of behavior are not overly simplistic or reductionist.

Conclusion

The "Karen" phenomenon, while offering valuable insights into modern societal dynamics, is not without its flaws. Its inherent gender bias reflects broader gender dynamics and stereotypes that have persisted through time. Addressing these biases requires introspection, education, and a commitment to seeing beyond labels. By doing so, society can foster an environment where behavior is critiqued constructively without resorting to gendered or oversimplified labels.

Highlighting "Ken" Moments and Comparing them to "Karen" Moments

While the "Karen" meme and the behaviors it lampoons have become deeply entrenched in the popular culture lexicon, there's an important counterpart to consider: the "Ken." While "Ken" moments may not have gained as much traction or notoriety as their female counterpart, they shed light on the gender dynamics and societal expectations at play. This section will highlight the nature of "Ken" moments and contrast them with "Karen" moments, underscoring the broader discourse on gendered behavior and societal perceptions.

The Nature of "Ken" Moments

"Ken" moments, named after the typical American male moniker, symbolize entitled, rude, or arrogant behaviors exhibited by men. Such incidents may involve:

- **Asserting Dominance:** Whether it's road rage incidents, confrontations in public spaces, or asserting perceived rights, "Kens" often operate under the belief that their stance or opinion holds dominion.
- **Mansplaining:** This is when men condescendingly explain something to someone, typically a woman, on a topic she is already familiar with or even an expert in.
- **Taking Up Space:** The act of "manspreading" in public transportation or the entitlement to physical and metaphorical space can be seen as a "Ken" behavior.

The Contrast: "Ken" vs. "Karen"

While both "Ken" and "Karen" behaviors revolve around entitlement and ignorance, the manifestations and societal reactions differ:

- **Intensity and Violence:** "Ken" moments, given societal stereotypes around male aggression, can sometimes lean more towards physical intimidation or overt aggression compared to "Karen" incidents.
- **Perceived Threat:** A confrontational "Ken" might be perceived as a more immediate physical threat than a "Karen," given societal beliefs about male strength and aggression.
- **Societal Repercussions:** "Karens" often face societal backlash rooted in gendered expectations about how women should behave (quiet, polite, non-confrontational). In contrast, "Kens," while criticized, might not face the same degree of gendered

backlash. Their behavior might sometimes be dismissed with phrases like "boys will be boys."

The Gender Dynamics at Play

Understanding "Ken" moments requires delving into the gendered expectations society holds:

- **Masculinity and Entitlement:** Traditional notions of masculinity often equate it with dominance, authority, and entitlement. These beliefs can inadvertently fuel "Ken" behaviors, with some men believing they have a right to assert, dominate, or explain.
- **Male Privilege:** Just as white privilege plays into many "Karen" incidents, male privilege underpins "Ken" behaviors. The ingrained belief that men have an inherent right to spaces, voices, and authority can manifest in confrontational or entitled actions.

The Media's Role

Much like "Karen" incidents, "Ken" moments gain traction through media and social platforms. However, the representation differs:

- **"Ken" as a Threat:** Media often portrays aggressive men as threats, focusing on the danger they pose. In contrast, "Karens" might be ridiculed or mocked for their perceived irrationality.
- **Limited Virality:** While "Karen" moments often go viral, gaining massive online traction, "Ken" incidents might not achieve the same level of virality. This disparity could be attributed to societal desensitization to male aggression or the lack of a cohesive, humorous narrative like the "Karen" stereotype.

Moving Beyond Gendered Labels

While understanding and analyzing "Ken" and "Karen" behaviors are essential, it's equally vital to move beyond these gendered labels:

- **Individual Accountability:** Instead of resorting to gendered stereotypes, holding individuals accountable for their actions irrespective of gender promotes a more nuanced understanding.

- **Challenge Gendered Expectations:** By questioning societal norms about how men and women "should" behave, society can break free from restrictive labels and allow for a fuller expression of individual personalities.

Conclusion

"Ken" moments, though less spotlighted than "Karen" incidents, offer valuable insights into gender dynamics, societal expectations, and the manifestation of entitlement. By comparing and contrasting these behaviors, society can better understand the gendered nuances of confrontation, entitlement, and privilege. Ultimately, moving beyond these labels and understanding the deeper issues at play is the way forward for a more inclusive and understanding society.

Chapter 6: Racial and Socioeconomic Dimensions

Examining Instances where Entitlement Intersects with Racial Prejudice

The "Karen" phenomenon, while deeply rooted in entitlement, often transcends just individual privilege. It has frequently intersected with racial prejudice, adding another layer of complexity and societal implications. This chapter aims to dissect instances where entitlement melds with racial bias, revealing the deeper systemic issues that underlie such incidents.

The Entitlement of "Whiteness"

Before delving into specific instances, it's essential to understand the concept of "white privilege." This societal advantage that benefits white individuals over non-white individuals in certain societies, particularly in areas like social, economic, and political life, inadvertently fosters a sense of entitlement.

- **Implicit Bias:** Years of racial stereotypes and biases have subconsciously informed public perceptions. Such biases might manifest in white individuals feeling threatened by a person of color without any substantial reason.

- **Societal Structures:** Historically, many societies have been structured to privilege white individuals. Such systemic advantages can create an unconscious sense of superiority or entitlement over individuals of other races.

Notable Instances of Racial Entitlement

Several instances have gained media attention, wherein white entitlement intersects with racial prejudice:

1. **Central Park Incident:** In 2020, a white woman called the police on a Black bird-watcher, falsely claiming he was threatening her. The situation arose from her feeling entitled to leash her dog in a leash-only area. However, when confronted by a Black individual, her entitlement mingled with racial bias, escalating the situation.

2. **Neighborhood Watch:** There have been countless instances where people of color, especially Black individuals, have been reported to the police for merely existing in predominantly white neighborhoods. The underlying entitlement here is the belief that these neighborhoods are "white spaces," and people of color are out of place or potential threats.

3. **Public Spaces:** From BBQs to swimming pools, there have been instances where white individuals have confronted people of color, questioning their right to access public spaces or partake in public activities. The entitlement here stems from a belief that these public spaces are implicitly "white spaces."

Socioeconomic Factors

The intersection of racial prejudice and entitlement isn't just about color but also involves socioeconomic factors:

- **Class and Race:** In many societies, race and class are intertwined. Stereotypes associating people of color with poverty, crime, or lower socioeconomic status exacerbate entitlement incidents, with white individuals sometimes feeling superior due to perceived socioeconomic advantages.

- **Gentrification:** As urban areas undergo redevelopment, long-time residents, often people of color, find themselves pushed out. New, often white, residents might exhibit entitlement, treating original inhabitants as outsiders or threats.

The Danger of Racially-Charged Entitlement

When entitlement intersects with racial prejudice, the consequences can be dire:

- **Escalation to Violence:** Situations can escalate, leading to physical harm. The belief in white superiority or the "threat" of people of color can lead to violent confrontations.

- **Systemic Support:** Often, systems, whether it's the police or neighborhood associations, might implicitly support the entitled individual, further endangering people of color.

- **Emotional and Psychological Trauma:** For people of color on the receiving end, these confrontations can lead to lasting emotional and psychological scars, reinforcing the societal message of their "lesser" status.

Addressing Racial Entitlement

Countering such racially-charged entitlement incidents involves multi-faceted approaches:

- **Education and Awareness:** It's essential to educate individuals about white privilege and the systemic advantages it offers. Recognizing privilege is the first step towards countering it.

- **Amplify Voices:** Giving platforms to people of color, allowing them to share their experiences, humanizes them, breaking down ingrained stereotypes.

- **Systemic Changes:** Institutions, from the police to schools, need to acknowledge racial biases and work towards creating more inclusive and fair systems.

Conclusion

The intersection of entitlement with racial prejudice magnifies the "Karen" phenomenon, revealing deeper societal fissures. By understanding these dynamics, society can work towards creating more inclusive spaces, ensuring that confrontations based on entitlement and racial biases become a thing of the past.

Discussing How Socio-Economic Factors May Amplify or Diminish "Karen" Behavior

Entitlement, ignorance, and assertive behavior—hallmarks of the "Karen" phenomenon—are not just grounded in gender or racial dynamics. Socioeconomic factors play a pivotal role in shaping these behaviors. By examining the impact of socioeconomic backgrounds and statuses on "Karen" behaviors, we can gain a more comprehensive understanding of the forces at play.

The Role of Socioeconomic Status (SES)

Socioeconomic status, often determined by factors like income, education, and occupation, can significantly influence individuals' worldviews, beliefs, and interactions. Those from a higher SES background may be more insulated from certain societal issues, fostering a sense of privilege and entitlement.

- **Insularity from Challenges:** Individuals from affluent backgrounds might be insulated from everyday challenges faced by those from lower SES. This insularity can breed a lack of empathy or understanding, manifesting as entitled behavior when confronted with situations outside their comfort zone.

- **Access to Resources:** Higher SES can provide individuals with more resources, from legal to financial, reinforcing their belief that they can act without repercussions.

Amplification of "Karen" Behavior by Higher SES

Higher socioeconomic status can sometimes amplify "Karen" behaviors:

- **Expectation of Preferential Treatment:** People from affluent backgrounds may expect a certain level of service or treatment. When these expectations are not met, it can lead to confrontations or demands for special treatment.

- **Lack of Consequences:** With financial resources or social connections at their disposal, individuals might feel they can act without facing repercussions. This belief can embolden entitled behaviors, as they feel shielded from consequences.

- **Social Bubbles:** Being surrounded by others from similar socioeconomic backgrounds can create an echo chamber, reinforcing certain beliefs and behaviors. Without diverse interactions, these individuals might lack a broader societal understanding.

Diminishing Effects of Higher SES

Conversely, higher socioeconomic status can also diminish "Karen" behaviors in certain contexts:

- **Education and Awareness:** Higher education levels, often associated with higher SES, can foster greater awareness of societal issues, including privilege and entitlement. Educated individuals might be more self-aware, preventing "Karen" behaviors.

- **Global Exposure:** Affluence can lead to increased travel or global exposure. Interacting with diverse cultures and societies can provide a broader perspective, curbing narrow-mindedness or entitlement.

Lower SES and "Karen" Behavior

While much of the "Karen" discourse focuses on individuals from higher SES backgrounds, it's crucial to understand how lower socioeconomic factors might influence such behaviors:

- **Struggle and Assertion:** People from lower SES backgrounds face numerous societal challenges. In some contexts, assertiveness (which can be mistaken for "Karen" behavior) might be a survival mechanism, ensuring they aren't overlooked or mistreated.

- **Misperceptions:** In certain scenarios, individuals from lower SES backgrounds might be perceived as entitled or confrontational when they're merely advocating for their rights. This misperception can be fueled by societal biases against those from lower economic backgrounds.

Intersection of SES with Race

Socioeconomic factors often intersect with racial dynamics, creating a layered effect:

- **Racial Wealth Gap:** Historical and systemic factors have led to significant wealth disparities between racial groups. A person of color exhibiting "Karen" behaviors might be navigating both racial prejudice and socioeconomic biases.

- **Stereotypes:** Stereotypes associating certain racial groups with poverty can amplify perceptions of entitlement or confrontational behavior, even if the individual is from a higher SES.

The Path Forward: Understanding Beyond Stereotypes

To move beyond the "Karen" stereotype and understand the nuances at play, it's essential to:

- **Acknowledge Socioeconomic Biases:** Recognizing that SES biases influence perceptions can lead to a more balanced understanding of confrontational or entitled behaviors.

- **Promote Socioeconomic Mobility:** Addressing the root causes, including systemic barriers to economic mobility, can reduce the chasm between different SES groups, promoting more harmonious interactions.

- **Education and Dialogue:** Encouraging dialogues around privilege, entitlement, and socioeconomic factors can foster understanding and empathy.

Conclusion

Socioeconomic factors significantly influence the manifestation and perceptions of "Karen" behaviors. By understanding these nuances, society can move beyond simplistic labels, fostering a more inclusive and empathetic environment.

Chapter 7:
The Aftermath

Real-life Consequences for Those Who Become Internet-Famous as a "Karen"

The digital age, characterized by the omnipresence of social media and the rapid dissemination of information, has radically transformed the landscape of public shaming. Individuals, once anonymous in their daily lives, can quickly become internet-infamous, subject to the gaze and judgment of millions. One such manifestation of this phenomenon is the "Karen" meme. However, what happens when the meme becomes real? What are the consequences for those who, willingly or unwittingly, step into the spotlight as a "Karen"?

The Immediate Fallout: Digital Shaming

Once a video or post depicting "Karen"-like behavior goes viral, the individual in question often faces a barrage of online criticism:

1. **Social Media Backlash:** Comments, shares, and reactions can range from mockery to outright hostility. The individual might receive thousands of negative messages, critiques, and, in extreme cases, threats.

2. **Personal Information Leaks:** Known as "doxxing," this dangerous tactic involves revealing the individual's personal information, from home addresses to workplace details, exacerbating the backlash.

3. **Meme-ification:** The individual's likeness might be transformed into memes, gifs, or other shareable content, reinforcing their "Karen" persona and making it harder to move past the incident.

Professional Repercussions

The ramifications aren't just limited to the digital realm. These incidents can spill into an individual's professional life:

- **Job Losses:** Employers, wary of negative publicity or disagreeing with the employee's actions, might terminate their employment. Several individuals labeled as "Karen" have lost their jobs after their incidents went viral.

- **Reputation Damage:** Professionals, especially those in client-facing roles or owning businesses, might experience a drop in clientele or face boycotts due to their newfound infamy.

- **Future Employment Challenges:** Future employers, upon discovering the viral incident, might be hesitant to hire the individual, fearing negative publicity or disruptive workplace dynamics.

Emotional and Psychological Impact

The emotional toll of becoming internet-infamous can be profound:

- **Mental Health Strain:** Facing a barrage of criticism and hate can lead to feelings of anxiety, depression, and isolation. The individual might feel overwhelmed, trapped, and vilified without an avenue for redemption.

- **Personal Relationships:** Relationships can become strained, with friends or family distancing themselves to avoid negative associations or confrontations regarding the incident.

- **Fear for Safety:** In extreme cases, where personal details are leaked or threats are made, the individual might fear for their physical safety.

Nuanced Cases and Redemption

While many "Karen" incidents depict clear-cut cases of entitlement or prejudice, some situations might be more nuanced:

- **Mental Health or Medical Issues:** Some individuals, post-backlash, have cited medical conditions or mental health crises as reasons for their outbursts. While this doesn't excuse the behavior, it adds layers of complexity to the situation.

- **Apologies and Growth:** Some individuals, upon reflection, have publicly apologized for their actions. They have undertaken measures, from attending workshops to therapy, to address and rectify their behavior.

Societal Implications: The Mob Mentality

While individuals who exhibit entitled or prejudiced behaviors must be held accountable, the aftermath of these incidents prompts broader societal questions:

- **Proportional Response:** Is the massive backlash, often involving thousands of strangers, a proportional response to the individual's actions? While holding individuals accountable is vital, there's a fine line between constructive criticism and destructive shaming.

- **Opportunity for Growth:** Does the digital backlash offer the individual an opportunity for growth and reflection, or does it push them further into their beliefs, creating a defensive stance?

- **Reflecting on Society:** Each "Karen" incident is a mirror to society, reflecting deep-seated beliefs, prejudices, and structures. Instead of focusing solely on the individual, there's an opportunity for society to introspect, addressing systemic issues that give rise to such behaviors.

Conclusion

The aftermath of becoming a "Karen" in the digital age is multifaceted, with professional, emotional, and societal implications. While it's crucial to hold individuals accountable, it's equally essential to ensure responses are proportional and constructive. By focusing on growth, education, and systemic change, society can move beyond the cycle of shaming towards a more empathetic and inclusive future.

Potential Benefits and Drawbacks of Public Shaming

Public shaming, an age-old societal tool of discipline, has been dramatically magnified in the age of the internet and social media. What was once a localized method to maintain community standards has now become a global spectacle. With the "Karen" phenomenon serving as a prominent example, it is critical to understand the broader implications, both positive and negative, of public shaming in the modern era.

Benefits of Public Shaming

Public shaming can act as a deterrent, a corrective mechanism, and a form of societal justice. Some of the benefits include:

1. **Accountability:** In instances where formal legal or administrative actions might be lacking, public shaming can hold individuals accountable for their actions, ensuring that they face consequences.

2. **Deterrence:** The fear of public humiliation can deter individuals from engaging in undesirable behaviors, thereby acting as a preventive measure.

3. **Public Awareness:** High-profile shaming incidents can raise awareness about particular issues, from racism to entitlement. This can lead to broader societal dialogues and introspection.

4. **Empowerment:** For victims or marginalized groups, public shaming can be a tool to reclaim power and highlight injustice. It offers a platform for voices that might otherwise be subdued or overlooked.

5. **Community Standards:** Public shaming can define and reinforce community standards. By collectively condemning

certain actions, communities can outline their values and expected behaviors.

Drawbacks of Public Shaming

Despite its potential benefits, public shaming has a range of adverse consequences, many of which can be disproportionate or long-lasting:

1. **Disproportional Punishment:** The intense, global nature of internet shaming can lead to punishments that far outweigh the transgression. A momentary lapse in judgment can lead to lasting infamy.

2. **Impact on Mental Health:** The subjects of public shaming can experience severe psychological distress, including depression, anxiety, and suicidal thoughts. The onslaught of negative attention can be overwhelming.

3. **Lack of Nuance:** Internet shaming often lacks nuance. Without the full context, individuals can be judged based on a single, isolated incident, which might not reflect their overall character or intentions.

4. **Mob Mentality:** Public shaming can fuel a mob mentality, where individuals participate in the shaming without fully understanding the context or considering the consequences of their actions.

5. **Potential for Mistakes:** There have been instances where the wrong individuals were targeted or where misrepresented information led to unwarranted backlash. Correcting such mistakes after the fact can be challenging.

6. **Endless Loop of Punishment:** In the digital age, mistakes are immortalized. Even after serving their "sentence," individuals might continuously face repercussions, as the internet doesn't easily forget.

Public Shaming and the "Karen" Phenomenon

The "Karen" meme exemplifies the complexities of public shaming:

- **Highlighting Prejudice:** Many "Karen" videos highlight genuine instances of racism, entitlement, and prejudice. Public shaming, in these cases, brings these issues to the forefront, forcing society to confront and address them.

- **Perpetuating Stereotypes:** On the flip side, the "Karen" label, when applied indiscriminately, can perpetuate gendered stereotypes. Not every demanding or assertive woman is a "Karen," and conflating the two can be problematic.

- **Redemption and Growth:** Some individuals, after facing public backlash, have shown genuine remorse and growth. Public shaming, in these cases, acted as a catalyst for positive change.

- **Unintended Consequences:** However, there have also been instances where the "Karen" label was misapplied or where the backlash was so severe that it led to disproportionate consequences, including job losses, threats, and severe emotional distress.

Navigating the Complexities

Given the mixed outcomes of public shaming, it's essential to navigate its complexities with care:

- **Informed Participation:** Before participating in or endorsing a shaming campaign, individuals should seek a comprehensive understanding of the context.

- **Proportional Response:** Efforts should be made to ensure that the backlash is proportional to the transgression. A balanced, measured response can prevent undue harm.

- **Focus on Education:** Instead of merely condemning, there's an opportunity to educate and foster understanding. Constructive dialogues can lead to lasting, positive change.

Conclusion

Public shaming, while a powerful tool for societal accountability and change, is fraught with challenges. Its double-edged nature, especially evident in the "Karen" phenomenon, underscores the need for thoughtful, informed, and empathetic engagement. As society becomes increasingly interconnected, it's more crucial than ever to wield the tool of public shaming with care, ensuring it promotes justice without perpetuating harm.

Chapter 8: Positive Spin-offs

Stories of Individuals Who've Used Their "Karen" Moments as a Wake-up Call

The "Karen" meme, while rooted in derision and public shaming, has had unintended positive outcomes for some individuals. Beneath the veneer of viral videos and internet ridicule, there are tales of introspection, growth, and transformation. Here, we delve into a few stories where individuals, once labeled as "Karen", chose to use their moment of internet infamy as a catalyst for personal change.

Rebecca's Realization

Rebecca, a businesswoman from New York, became the face of entitlement when she was filmed berating a barista over a trivial mistake in her coffee order. The video, highlighting her use of profanities and threats, went viral overnight. But rather than retreating into defensiveness, Rebecca publicly apologized. More importantly, she sought therapy to address her underlying anger issues. Months later, she started a support group for individuals dealing with anger management, turning her moment of shame into a platform for healing both herself and others.

Melanie's Move

Melanie's confrontation with her neighbor over a property dispute became the talk of the internet. Accused of being racially prejudiced, she was termed a "Karen". Stunned by this label and deeply introspective, Melanie enrolled in cultural sensitivity and anti-racism workshops. This journey led her to volunteer in community integration projects, where she now actively works to bridge cultural and racial divides.

Sarah's Second Chance

Sarah, a teacher from Texas, faced severe backlash after being filmed shouting at a student for what appeared to be a minor misbehavior. Labeled a "Karen", she faced immense scrutiny, both online and offline. Sarah chose to see this as a wake-up call. She took a sabbatical, traveling to different countries to teach under-privileged children. Along the way, she learned patience, empathy, and the true essence of teaching. Returning home, she became an advocate for teacher training programs that focused on emotional intelligence and relationship-building.

David's Detour

While the "Karen" label is predominantly associated with women, men aren't exempt. David, a "Ken", was captured on camera aggressively confronting a teenager for skateboarding in a no-skate zone. The video, highlighting his authoritative and demeaning tone, went viral. David, a former skateboarder himself, was forced to confront his hypocritical stance. In an attempt to right his wrongs, he collaborated with local authorities to create a skate park for teenagers, ensuring they had a safe space to pursue their passion.

Lisa's Learning

Lisa, once an internet sensation for her tantrum over a missed flight, chose introspection over indignation. Recognizing her entitled behavior, she sought to understand its roots. This led her to volunteer in countries with limited resources, where she experienced firsthand the challenges many face in their daily lives. These experiences humbled her, providing perspective on her own privileges. Lisa now runs workshops in schools, teaching children the value of gratitude and perspective.

A Broader Perspective

While these stories highlight personal journeys of growth, they also underscore a broader societal lesson. Each "Karen" moment, no matter how seemingly trivial, reflects deep-seated beliefs, prejudices, and entitlements. These instances aren't isolated but are part of a larger tapestry of societal dynamics.

However, transformation is possible. As seen in the stories above, individuals can choose introspection over indignation. They can leverage their moments of shame as catalysts for growth, turning negative attention into positive action.

The Role of Society

Society plays a pivotal role in these transformations. The reaction to "Karen" incidents can range from constructive criticism to destructive shaming. For individuals to truly grow and evolve, they need a supportive environment that fosters understanding, education, and redemption.

Conclusion

The "Karen" meme, while a tool of mockery and shaming, has the potential to be a tool for change. The onus lies both with individuals, to recognize and rectify their behaviors, and with society, to provide a conducive environment for such transformations. In the midst of viral videos and internet ridicule, there lies an opportunity for growth, understanding, and positive change.

Communities and Online Spaces Helping Educate and Reform Entitled Behavior

In the age of the internet, public shaming often feels like the norm. While the "Karen" meme serves as a prime example of such shaming, it also underscores the power of online communities. Beneath the surface of viral videos and biting humor, there exists a parallel narrative: one where the online world offers education, understanding, and reformation. Various communities and spaces have emerged, focusing on helping individuals recognize entitled behavior and fostering positive change.

1. Online Forums for Open Dialogue

Platforms like Reddit and Quora have become vital spaces where individuals can engage in meaningful discussions about behavior, entitlement, and societal norms. Subreddits such as r/AmItheAsshole offer users a chance to post personal stories and get feedback on whether their actions were justified or out of line. Such platforms provide a mix of perspectives, enabling individuals to see situations from different viewpoints and reflect on their behaviors.

2. Therapeutic Communities

The rise of online therapy platforms has been complemented by communities dedicated to self-improvement and mental health awareness. These spaces emphasize understanding the root causes of entitled behavior, often linking them to deeper psychological issues or past traumas. They offer resources, coping mechanisms, and professional guidance to those willing to address and rectify their behaviors.

3. Cultural Sensitivity Workshops

The internet has democratized access to education. Many "Karen" incidents revolve around racial or cultural insensitivity. Recognizing this, numerous online platforms offer courses, webinars, and workshops focused on cultural understanding, anti-racism, and inclusivity. Websites like Coursera and Udemy host courses designed by experts to help individuals broaden their perspectives and foster global understanding.

4. Mindfulness and Meditation Groups

Entitled behavior often stems from unchecked emotions or a lack of self-awareness. Online communities centered around mindfulness and meditation have emerged as vital resources. Platforms like Insight Timer or Headspace not only offer guided meditations but also have community features where users can discuss their journeys, challenges, and personal growth stories.

5. Support Groups

The realization of one's entitled behavior can be daunting, leading to feelings of shame, guilt, or isolation. Online support groups, available on platforms like Facebook or specialized forums, provide a safe space for individuals to share their stories, seek advice, and embark on their reformation journeys together.

6. Educational Videos and Content Creators

YouTube, TikTok, and similar platforms have a plethora of content creators who focus on educating their audience about societal norms, entitled behaviors, and the importance of empathy. By using humor, storytelling, and facts, these creators break down complex topics, making them accessible and relatable. They not only highlight the issues but also offer solutions and pathways to personal growth.

7. Constructive Feedback Platforms

Websites like ConstructiveCritics.com allow users to anonymously post about their actions and receive constructive feedback. Such platforms prioritize education over shaming, ensuring that users get a balanced view of their behaviors and practical advice on how to change.

8. Reading and Book Clubs

Online book clubs, focusing on topics of personal growth, empathy, and societal understanding, have gained traction. Platforms like Goodreads have communities where members read, discuss, and reflect upon literature that can offer insights into human behavior and the roots of entitlement.

The Impact of These Communities

While the internet can be a hub of negativity, these communities highlight its potential as a force for good. They offer:

- **Safe Spaces:** Individuals can learn, make mistakes, seek feedback, and grow without fear of undue judgment or ridicule.
- **Diverse Perspectives:** Online communities are global, ensuring that individuals are exposed to a plethora of viewpoints, enriching their understanding.
- **Accessibility:** The democratizing power of the internet ensures that resources for personal growth are accessible to all, regardless of geographical or financial constraints.
- **Peer Learning:** Instead of a top-down approach, these communities often emphasize peer learning, where members learn from each other's experiences and insights.

Conclusion

In the midst of memes and viral videos, the internet's potential to foster understanding, education, and growth shines through. For every "Karen" shamed, there's an opportunity for reflection, learning, and positive change. And with the help of dedicated online communities and platforms, more and more individuals are finding paths to self-awareness and transformation.

Chapter 9: Countering the 'Karen' Epidemic

Strategies for Dealing with Entitled Behavior in Public

The proliferation of "Karen" incidents in public places underscores a broader societal issue: how do we effectively and empathetically deal with entitled behavior when confronted with it? Addressing such behavior requires tact, patience, and an understanding of the underlying dynamics. Here, we delve into strategies that can be employed when facing entitlement in public spaces.

1. Stay Calm and Collected

One of the most effective ways to respond to entitled behavior is by remaining calm. Entitlement often seeks validation through confrontation. By staying composed, you're less likely to escalate the situation. Taking deep breaths and reminding oneself to stay grounded can prevent reactive responses.

2. Active Listening

Sometimes, what appears as entitled behavior may be a result of underlying frustration or misunderstanding. By actively listening to the individual's grievances, you signal respect and understanding. This can often de-escalate tensions and pave the way for constructive dialogue.

3. Assertive Communication

Being calm doesn't mean being passive. It's essential to communicate your boundaries and feelings assertively. Using "I" statements, such as "I understand where you're coming from, but I feel uncomfortable with this behavior," can be effective in expressing your stance without appearing confrontational.

4. Seek Mediation

In situations where tensions are high, seeking a neutral third party can help. This could be a security officer, a manager, or any other authority figure in the vicinity. Their presence can often neutralize the situation, and their perspective can provide a balanced resolution.

5. Disengage When Necessary

Not all confrontations are worth engaging in. If someone's entitled behavior poses a threat to your well-being or safety, it's crucial to prioritize self-preservation. Removing yourself from the situation or seeking help if you feel threatened is essential.

6. Educate, If Openness is Perceived

In cases where the individual displays ignorance rather than malice, there may be an opportunity for education. Share resources, articles, or personal experiences that can shed light on the issue at hand. However, it's vital to gauge the individual's openness to such dialogue. If they're defensive or aggressive, it's best to refrain.

7. Document If Necessary

With the rise of smartphones, documentation has become an effective tool in holding entitled individuals accountable. If you believe someone's behavior is crossing ethical or legal boundaries, recording the incident (where legally permissible) can serve as evidence if needed later.

8. Reflect on Your Role

It's essential to introspect and assess if there's anything in your behavior that might have unintentionally provoked or escalated the situation. While this isn't to blame the victim, understanding one's actions can offer insights into how similar situations can be avoided or better managed in the future.

9. Seek Support Post-Encounter

Dealing with entitled individuals can be emotionally taxing. After such an encounter, it's crucial to seek support, whether from friends, family, or professionals. Sharing your experience and feelings can provide relief and perspective.

10. Promote Awareness and Education

One of the ways to counter the "Karen" epidemic is by fostering societal awareness. Engage in community discussions, workshops, and seminars that address entitled behavior. The more people are aware of its detrimental effects, the more proactive the community becomes in curbing it.

The Broader Perspective

While these strategies offer individual ways to counter entitled behavior, there's a broader societal role to play. Institutions, businesses, and community leaders can set clear guidelines and codes of conduct that define acceptable behavior in public spaces. Training staff in conflict resolution, promoting awareness campaigns, and fostering community dialogue can go a long way in creating environments that discourage entitlement.

Conclusion

Dealing with entitlement requires a balance of assertiveness, empathy, and understanding. While it's challenging to navigate such confrontations, equipped with the right strategies, individuals can effectively address "Karen" behaviors. Moreover, as society becomes more aware of the detrimental effects of entitlement, collective efforts can pave the way for more respectful and understanding public interactions.

Personal Stories from People Who've Diffused Tense Situations

Entitled behavior, often embodied by the "Karen" stereotype, can create challenging situations for bystanders, employees, or anyone caught in its crosshairs. While the internet is filled with videos of such confrontations escalating, there are countless unsung stories of individuals who've successfully diffused these situations with tact, empathy, and quick thinking. Let's dive into some of these stories.

1. Sarah's Coffee Shop Conundrum

Sarah, a barista at a local coffee shop, encountered a woman irate about her drink order. Instead of matching the woman's intensity, Sarah listened patiently, repeating back what she understood to ensure she grasped the issue. Recognizing the woman's need to feel heard, Sarah's calm demeanor eventually led the woman to apologize for her outburst. By validating the woman's feelings, Sarah turned a potential confrontation into a teachable moment.

2. Michael's Parking Space Peace

Michael recalls a time when he parked in a spot that another driver, a visibly frustrated man, claimed he'd been waiting for. Instead of engaging in an argument, Michael calmly acknowledged the man's frustration and offered to find another spot. Michael says, "It wasn't about conceding; it was about recognizing that a parking space wasn't worth the escalation." His humility prevented a potential roadside altercation.

3. Amina's Restaurant Resolution

Amina, a restaurant manager, dealt with a customer who loudly complained about the wait time. Noting that other patrons were getting uncomfortable, Amina approached the table with a friend-ly demeanor, validating the customer's feelings about waiting. She then offered a complimentary appetizer for the table as a goodwill gesture. Her recognition of the customer's impatience, combined with a proactive solution, quickly defused the tension.

4. Raj's Supermarket Standoff

While queuing at the supermarket, Raj found himself confronted by a woman who believed he had skipped the line. Instead of getting defensive, Raj decided to engage her in light conversation, distracting from the initial issue. By the time they reached the checkout, the two were discussing their favorite foods, and the initial disagreement was forgotten. Raj's strategy of redirecting the conversation transformed a potential conflict into a friendly exchange.

5. Elena's Gym Grace

Elena recalls a situation at her gym where a fellow member aggressively confronted her for using a machine "too long." Recognizing the woman's heightened emotions, Elena chose to respond with kindness. She complimented the woman's workout regimen and asked for tips. This unexpected kindness caught the woman off guard, leading her to apologize for her outburst. Elena's choice to counter aggression with kindness changed the trajectory of the interaction.

6. Liam's Library Lesson

Liam, a librarian, once dealt with a patron angrily challenging a late fee. Instead of reiterating the rules, Liam asked the man about the book he'd borrowed and if he had enjoyed it. This shift in focus led the man to talk passionately about the novel, and in the process, he cooled down. Liam then calmly explained the late fee's necessity, to which the man willingly complied. By redirecting the focus and finding common ground, Liam transformed a confrontational scenario.

7. Isabella's Flight Fix

On an overbooked flight, Isabella found herself face-to-face with a man claiming she was in his seat. With tensions high, Isabella calmly asked a flight attendant for assistance and struck up a conversation with the man about their destinations. Discovering they were both headed to the same conference, their conversation shifted to shared interests. By the time the seating issue was resolved, the two had exchanged business cards, turning a conflict into a networking opportunity.

Lessons from the Frontlines

These stories underscore a few key takeaways:

- **Empathy First:** Recognizing and validating the emotions of the individual, even if they're misplaced, can de-escalate many situations.
- **Redirect and Distract:** Shifting the focus of the conversation can transform its trajectory.
- **Stay Calm:** Matching aggression with aggression rarely yields positive outcomes. Remaining calm and composed can influence the other party to do the same.

Conclusion

The "Karen" epidemic, with its heightened emotions and confrontations, can be challenging to navigate. However, as these personal stories highlight, with a mix of empathy, quick thinking, and genuine human connection, many of these situations can be defused, fostering understanding and, at times, even unlikely friendships.

Chapter 10: The Future of the 'Karen' Phenomenon

How Will the Meme Evolve as Society Changes?

The "Karen" meme, as with most cultural phenomena, is a reflection of societal dynamics at a given time. As societies evolve, so too will the symbols, jokes, and references they use to communicate shared understandings, frustrations, or critiques. The future of the "Karen" meme, like all memes, will be shaped by changing cultural, technological, and socio-political landscapes. Here, we explore potential trajectories for the evolution of the "Karen" phenomenon.

1. Societal Push Towards Empathy and Understanding

Modern societies are becoming increasingly aware of the importance of mental health, empathy, and understanding. As these values take precedence, there might be a shift in how we respond to "Karen" incidents. The meme could evolve from a tool of mockery to a symbol of the need for broader societal compassion, understanding that such outbursts might stem from deeper personal issues.

2. Expansion or Replacement with New Stereotypes

While "Karen" currently encapsulates a particular type of entitled behavior, stereotypes are continuously evolving. The meme could expand to encompass a broader range of behaviors or be replaced by newer stereotypes that reflect changing societal concerns.

3. A Shift to Global Contexts

With the world becoming increasingly interconnected, the "Karen" meme might adapt to global contexts. Entitled behaviors are not exclusive to any one culture, and as the meme finds resonance in various countries, it might morph to reflect localized interpretations of entitlement and privilege.

4. Decline Due to Overuse

Like many popular memes, the "Karen" meme might face decline due to overuse. As it becomes mainstream and is co-opted by various groups for different purposes, its original essence and impact might dilute, leading to its eventual fading from popular discourse.

5. Commercialization and Monetization

There's already evidence of the "Karen" meme being used in merchandise, from T-shirts to mugs. As with many viral concepts, there's potential for its commercialization to increase, which might change its perception from a tool of social critique to just another pop culture reference.

6. Policy and Legal Implications

Given the real-life consequences faced by some individuals labeled as "Karen" online, there might be future legal implications. Cyberbullying and online harassment laws could adapt to protect individuals from mass shaming, which might reduce the virality of such incidents and, by extension, the meme's prevalence.

7. Technological Influences

The platforms that host these "Karen" videos or discussions play a role in the meme's propagation. If platforms change their algorithms, policies, or user behaviors shift, it could influence how and where the "Karen" discourse happens. New technologies like augmented reality or virtual reality could also offer fresh platforms for the meme to evolve.

8. Reclamation and Ownership

Much like some marginalized groups have reclaimed derogatory terms, it's possible that those named Karen might reclaim the meme. It could become a symbol of self-awareness, with individuals using it humorously to acknowledge moments where they might have acted entitled or out of line.

9. Broader Societal Critiques

The "Karen" meme might evolve to encompass broader critiques of societal systems. Beyond just individual entitlement, it might come to symbolize systemic issues related to consumerism, privilege, or other macro-level concerns.

10. Documentary and Historical Analysis

As with many cultural phenomena of significance, the "Karen" meme might become a subject of documentary or academic interest. Future generations might study it to understand the societal dynamics of the early 21st century, much like we analyze literature, art, or media from previous eras to glean insights into those times.

Conclusion

The "Karen" meme, rooted in societal observations about entitlement and privilege, offers a snapshot of current cultural conversations. Its future evolution will undoubtedly be as dynamic as the society from which it emerged. Whether it fades, morphs, or remains a constant, its trajectory offers valuable insights into the ever-evolving nature of culture, technology, and societal values.

Potential Implications for Future Generations

As we delve into the cultural zeitgeist that the "Karen" meme represents, it's essential to consider the legacy it will leave for future generations. Memes, while often considered fleeting, can have profound effects on shaping societal attitudes, behaviors, and norms. The "Karen" meme, with its powerful commentary on entitlement, privilege, and public behavior, will undoubtedly cast a long shadow. Below, we explore the potential implications this phenomenon might have for the generations to come.

1. A Heightened Awareness of Entitlement and Privilege

The "Karen" meme has put a spotlight on behavior marked by entitlement and privilege. As a result, future generations might grow up with a keener awareness of these issues, leading to a society more attuned to recognizing and countering such attitudes.

2. A Changing Landscape of Accountability

In a world where actions can quickly become viral, future generations may adopt a heightened sense of public accountability. The "Karen" meme serves as a cautionary tale that one's behavior, especially in public settings, can have lasting digital footprints. This might foster a society where people think twice before acting impulsively or entitled.

3. Re-defining Digital Justice

For the generations growing up in the digital age, the "Karen" phenomenon provides essential lessons on digital justice. It poses essential questions: When does calling out become public shaming? Is it always justifiable to "cancel" someone based on a singular incident? These considerations might lead to more nuanced approaches to online justice, ensuring it's meted out more judiciously.

4. The Evolution of Memetic Literacy

Future generations might develop a more refined "memetic literacy"—an ability to decode, understand, and critique the cultural implications of memes. As memes like "Karen" play essential roles in social commentary, understanding their layers, origins, and implications becomes crucial for informed societal participation.

5. The Power and Peril of Stereotyping

While the "Karen" meme sheds light on specific behaviors, it also risks oversimplifying complex human actions into caricatures. Future generations might grapple with the balance between using stereotypes as communicative shortcuts and ensuring they don't perpetuate unfair or overly simplistic views of individuals.

6. Critical Consumption of Media

With the proliferation of "Karen" videos and discussions online, future generations will learn the importance of critical media consumption. They'll be tasked with discerning genuine incidents of entitlement from those taken out of context, or worse, staged for virality. This discernment will be a crucial skill in a media-saturated future.

7. A Re-evaluation of Privacy

The "Karen" meme often arises from real-life incidents caught on camera. This blurring of public and private lives might push future generations to re-evaluate the boundaries of privacy. They might advocate for clearer norms around what can be filmed, shared, or monetized, especially without the consent of all parties involved.

8. Emphasizing Empathy and Rehabilitation

As future generations witness the profound effects of being labeled a "Karen" on individuals' lives, there might be a shift towards emphasizing empathy and rehabilitation over ridicule and punishment. This could manifest in online platforms that focus on education and constructive dialogue rather than shaming.

9. A More Reflexive Culture

With memes like "Karen" holding a mirror to society, future generations might develop a more reflexive culture—constantly self-examining, checking biases, and striving for growth. This self-awareness could lead to societies that are quicker to acknowledge flaws and more proactive in addressing them.

10. Navigating the Intersectionality of Issues

The "Karen" meme touches on gender, race, class, and more. For future generations, it serves as a template for navigating the intersectionality of societal issues. They'll learn the importance of understanding problems in their multifaceted complexity rather than siloed simplicity.

Conclusion

The "Karen" phenomenon, far from being just a fleeting meme, holds profound implications for the generations that will follow. Its legacy lies not just in the behaviors it critiques but in the broader lessons it imparts about digital culture, accountability, empathy, and societal reflexivity. As future generations inherit this world, they'll be tasked with taking these lessons to heart, shaping a society that's not only aware of its flaws but actively strives to address them.

Conclusion

Reflection on the Broader Themes of Entitlement, Cultural Responsiveness, and the Power of Social Media

As we wrap up our exploration of the "Karen" phenomenon, it becomes evident that the issues encapsulated within this meme reach far beyond the confines of a viral trend. Delving into the "Karen" meme is not just about understanding one particular stereotype; it's about reflecting upon broader themes of entitlement, cultural responsiveness, and the immense power of social media in today's age. Let's unpack these themes and understand their wider implications.

1. Entitlement: A Historical and Contemporary Analysis

The "Karen" meme's foundation is the portrayal of entitlement—a belief that one deserves certain privileges, irrespective of one's behavior or the situational context. Historically, entitlement has roots in power dynamics, often linked with socioeconomic status, race, and gender. While feudal lords and monarchs in the past exhibited overt entitlement, today, this attitude has subtly permeated various facets of society.

Modern entitlement can manifest in myriad ways—from a customer demanding undue privileges in a store to someone feeling they have the right to police public spaces based on personal biases. Such behaviors, as the "Karen" meme highlights, can lead to interpersonal conflicts and exacerbate societal divides. Thus, understanding and curbing entitlement becomes crucial in fostering a more harmonious society.

2. Cultural Responsiveness: From Ignorance to Awareness

The "Karen" phenomenon also brings to the fore the importance of cultural responsiveness—the ability to understand, communicate with, and effectively interact with people from various cultural backgrounds. Some "Karen" incidents, where racial bias is evident, highlight the glaring lack of cultural responsiveness in certain individuals.

For societies to thrive in an interconnected, globalized world, cultural responsiveness is non-negotiable. It calls for individuals to move beyond ignorance and stereotypes and embrace the rich tapestry of cultures that make up the world. Encounters labeled under the "Karen" meme can serve as cautionary tales, emphasizing the importance of cultural education, awareness, and sensitivity.

3. The Power of Social Media: Amplification and Accountability

One cannot discuss the "Karen" meme without acknowledging the role of social media. Platforms like Twitter, Instagram, TikTok, and Facebook have amplified individual incidents to global audiences, demonstrating the immense power of these digital spaces.

On the one hand, this amplification brings accountability. People exhibiting entitled or prejudiced behavior know that their actions could have wider repercussions. This public form of accountability can act as a deterrent, encouraging individuals to reflect on and modify their behavior.

However, on the flip side, the power of social media also poses risks. The speed at which content spreads means that context often gets lost, leading to misinterpretations. Additionally, public shaming on such a vast scale can have severe mental health repercussions for the individuals involved—even if they were at fault. Thus, the power of social media is a double-edged sword: it can foster accountability but can also lead to undue vilification.

4. The Interplay of These Themes

The intersection of entitlement, cultural responsiveness, and the power of social media creates a complex web. Entitled behavior, when captured and shared, gets magnified by social media. The reactions to such behavior, ranging from supportive to extremely critical, reflect society's varying levels of cultural responsiveness.

This dynamic interplay underscores the importance of each individual's responsibility. It calls for self-awareness to ensure one doesn't exhibit undue entitlement. It emphasizes the need for continuous cultural education, ensuring one's actions are always respectful and informed. And finally, it serves as a reminder of the vast power of social media, urging individuals to use these platforms judiciously, both as content creators and consumers.

Final Thoughts

The "Karen" meme, while seemingly a product of internet culture, holds profound reflections on society's values, behaviors, and the mediums that shape our perceptions. As we move forward, it's essential to internalize the broader themes highlighted by this phenomenon. By doing so, we can hope for a world marked by lesser entitlement, greater cultural responsiveness, and a more thoughtful use of the immense power that social media wields.

A Call to Empathy and Understanding

As we navigate the digital age, the "Karen" meme stands as a testament to the complexities of human interaction in today's interconnected world. But beyond the viral videos, tweets, and online debates lies a more profound truth about human nature, communication, and the need for understanding. It's time to transition from mere spectators to proactive participants in shaping a more empathetic society.

1. The Power of Empathy in Difficult Situations

Empathy—the ability to understand and share the feelings of another—is often our most potent tool when confronting entitled or prejudiced behaviors. While it's easy to judge, mock, or even vilify individuals based on short video clips or stories, empathy calls for a more profound engagement.

By placing ourselves in the shoes of all parties involved—whether it's the person exhibiting "Karen" behavior or the individual on the receiving end—we gain a broader perspective. Recognizing that everyone has a backstory, that everyone has challenges and fears, can fundamentally shift our response from one of disdain to compassion. This doesn't mean excusing prejudiced or harmful behavior, but it does mean approaching situations with a genuine desire to understand rather than merely judge.

2. The Multiplicity of Human Emotion and Experience

It's crucial to remember that every individual is a product of their experiences, upbringing, and environment. Factors such as past traumas, stressors, or even mental health issues can profoundly influence behavior. The "Karen" we see in a two-minute video clip might be going through personal upheavals we cannot even fathom. This understanding doesn't justify any form of harm or prejudice they might perpetrate, but it provides context.

Similarly, the individuals who face entitled or prejudiced behavior carry their own stories, hopes, and fears. By recognizing the multiplicity of human emotion and experience, we can foster more meaningful connections and respond more holistically to conflicts.

3. The Role of Constructive Dialogue

One of the most effective antidotes to ignorance and prejudice is constructive dialogue. Instead of immediately condemning "Karen"-like behaviors, we can seek to initiate conversations. Ask questions. Share personal experiences. Educate. Often, ignorance is not a result of deep-rooted malice but a lack of awareness. Engaging in open dialogue can bridge gaps of understanding and can pave the way for personal growth and societal change.

4. Reimagining Digital Responsibility

With the power of social media comes immense responsibility. Before sharing, commenting on, or amplifying "Karen" incidents, it's essential to pause and reflect. What impact will sharing this content have on all parties involved? Is there a more constructive way to address the issue? Can we promote understanding and growth instead of further polarization?

Digital responsibility also means critically evaluating information, seeking context, and refraining from engaging in or promoting online mob mentality. By adopting a more measured, empathetic approach online, we can create digital spaces that promote understanding, education, and collective growth.

5. The Broader Societal Call to Action

As members of an interconnected global society, we all play a role in shaping its values, norms, and behaviors. Beyond individual interactions, there's a broader call to action to instill empathy and understanding as core societal values. This could mean integrating empathy training in educational curricula, promoting community dialogue initiatives, or even supporting mental health and well-being programs that help individuals navigate personal challenges.

Final Thoughts: Choosing the Path of Empathy

The "Karen" phenomenon offers more than mere entertainment or fleeting internet trends. It holds a mirror to society, reflecting both our challenges and our potential for growth. As we move forward, the choice lies with us. We can continue to perpetuate cycles of judgment, shaming, and polarization. Or, we can choose the path of empathy—seeking to understand, connect, and uplift.

In this interconnected world, our actions, both online and offline, have ripples. Let's ensure that these ripples spread understanding, compassion, and hope. It's time to transition from mere spectators to proactive advocates of empathy, understanding, and positive change.

Appendix A: Infamous "Karen" Videos and Their Backstories

The "Karen" meme reached its pinnacle of popularity through various viral videos, each illustrating a different shade of entitled or prejudiced behavior. As the meme permeated the cultural consciousness, these videos offered not just a moment of shock or humor, but also a glimpse into the deeper dynamics of societal conflicts. Let's take a closer look at some of the most infamous "Karen" videos and uncover the stories behind them.

1. Central Park Birdwatching Incident

This incident, which took place in May 2020, became one of the most widely-discussed examples of racial bias. Amy Cooper, a white woman, was walking her dog off-leash in an area of New York's Central Park where leashing was mandatory. Christian Cooper (no relation), an African American man and avid birdwatcher, requested her to leash her dog to not disturb the wildlife.

When she refused, he began filming. In the video, Amy becomes agitated and threatens to call the police and "tell them an African American man is threatening my life." She then proceeds to do so. The video quickly went viral, leading to discussions about weaponizing racial bias and white privilege.

Backstory: Amy Cooper faced significant repercussions, losing her job and temporarily surrendering her dog to a rescue organization. She later apologized for her actions. Christian Cooper emphasized the importance of addressing the underlying racial bias rather than focusing on individual punishment.

2. Starbucks Confrontation

In this viral video, a woman becomes upset when her Starbucks drink is not made to her exact specifications. She demands a refund and loudly berates the staff, making the video an archetype of the "entitled customer" Karen.

Backstory: While less political than some other "Karen" incidents, this video sparked discussions about the treatment of service workers and the undue expectations and entitlement some customers exhibit. Many service workers shared their own stories of dealing with difficult customers, highlighting a pervasive issue in customer service industries.

3. Store Mask Meltdown

During the COVID-19 pandemic, mask mandates were a contentious topic. In one video, a woman at a supermarket is seen throwing her shopping cart items onto the floor after being told she must wear a mask to shop. She shouts about her rights and her disapproval of the mandate.

Backstory: The widespread debates on personal freedoms versus public health regulations were the backdrop to many such videos during the pandemic. This specific video was emblematic of tensions and anxieties people felt during an unprecedented global crisis. The video sparked debates about personal responsibility during a public health emergency.

4. "Kid's Play" Playground Incident

A woman, later dubbed "Playground Karen," was filmed calling the police on a man who was accompanying his son to a local playground. She insisted that the man, who was of Hispanic descent, had no reason to be in a "kids' area" and implied he might be a threat.

Backstory: This incident shined a spotlight on the racial profiling many people of color experience in everyday situations. The man was simply spending a day at the park with his son, an activity any parent has the right to enjoy without suspicion. After the video went viral, the community rallied behind the man, condemning racial bias and profiling.

5. "BBQ Becky"

In 2018, a woman in Oakland, California, dubbed "BBQ Becky," called the police on two African American men for using a charcoal grill in a designated barbecue zone in a park. She insisted they were breaking the law, even though they were in a permitted area.

Backstory: The 25-minute video, which captured the woman's persistent attempts to report the men, became a symbol of racial bias and the unnecessary policing of Black individuals in public spaces. The incident resulted in a massive "BBQing While Black" event in the same park weeks later, where residents came together in solidarity against racial bias.

Conclusion

Each of these viral moments offers more than just a glimpse of confrontation. They provide insights into larger societal issues like racial bias, entitlement, and the treatment of service workers. While the "Karen" meme simplifies these incidents into digestible, often humorous snippets, the backstories demand a more profound reflection on societal values, biases, and the need for change.

Appendix B: Resources for Further Reading and Understanding

To gain a deeper understanding of the "Karen" phenomenon, its implications, and the broader cultural dynamics at play, it's essential to turn to a range of materials that delve into related subjects. Here, we've curated a list of books, articles, and other resources that can provide additional insight, historical context, and psychological perspectives on the topic.

Books

1. **"White Fragility: Why It's So Hard for White People to Talk About Racism" by Robin DiAngelo**

   DiAngelo provides a comprehensive examination of white fragility, exploring the defensive reactions many white individuals have when confronted with discussions about race. This book can offer valuable insights into some of the behaviors and attitudes exhibited by those dubbed "Karens."

2. **"So You Want to Talk About Race" by Ijeoma Oluo**

   Oluo's book is a forthright discussion on race, addressing topics such as privilege, intersectionality, and microaggressions. It's a must-read for anyone looking to understand the modern racial landscape in the U.S.

3. "The Age of Entitlement: America Since the Sixties" by Christopher Caldwell

Caldwell traces the origins and growth of entitlement in America, offering insights into how societal changes have fostered an era where entitlement is rampant.

4. "Dare to Lead: Brave Work. Tough Conversations. Whole Hearts." by Brené Brown

While not directly about the "Karen" meme, Brown's book is about vulnerability, leadership, and the courage to engage in difficult conversations, offering tools and strategies for effective communication.

Articles & Essays

1. "The Weaponization of White Womanhood" by Rachel Elizabeth Cargle (Harper's Bazaar)

Cargle examines the historical context of white women using their societal positioning to weaponize their emotions and fragility against people of color, specifically Black men.

2. "How 'Karen' Became a Symbol of Racism" by Aja Romano (Vox)

Romano's article provides a detailed exploration of the "Karen" meme's origin, its cultural significance, and its ties to racism and privilege.

3. "The Psychology Behind The 'Karen' Phenomenon" by Jessica Grogan (Psychology Today)

Grogan delves into the psychological motivations and factors that might contribute to "Karen-like" behavior, from entitlement to a lack of self-awareness.

Documentaries & Video Resources

1. "13th" directed by Ava DuVernay (Available on Netflix)

This powerful documentary offers an in-depth look at the history of racial inequality in the United States, focusing on the nation's prisons and how they are disproportionately filled with African-Americans.

2. **"The Social Dilemma"** directed by Jeff Orlowski (Available on Netflix)

While not exclusively about the "Karen" meme, this documentary dives deep into the world of social media, its algorithms, and how these platforms can amplify societal divisions.

3. **"Ted Talk: We need to talk about an injustice"** by Bryan Stevenson

Stevenson, a lawyer and social justice activist, gives a compelling talk about the racial disparities in America's justice system and the urgent need for reform.

Online Platforms & Communities

1. **Reddit: r/PublicFreakout & r/AmItheAsshole**

These subreddits often feature discussions and videos related to "Karen" incidents. They are communities where people share experiences, seek feedback, and discuss the societal implications of various confrontations.

2. **Instagram: @soyouwanttotalkabout**

This account offers slide-style posts discussing various societal issues, including racism, privilege, and cultural awareness. They have tackled the "Karen" phenomenon from multiple angles.

Conclusion

The "Karen" phenomenon offers a lens into deeper societal issues, from racial biases and entitlement to the impact of social media on public discourse. To understand the phenomenon's full breadth and depth, it's essential to dive into these resources and others. Engaging with these materials will equip readers with the knowledge to navigate discussions on the subject with empathy, awareness, and insight.